Minerals

by Grace Hansen

Abdo
GEOLOGY ROCKS!
Kids

abdopublishing.com

Published by Abdo Kids, a division of ABDO, PO Box 398166, Minneapolis, Minnesota 55439.

Copyright © 2016 by Abdo Consulting Group, Inc. International copyrights reserved in all countries. No part of this book may be reproduced in any form without written permission from the publisher.

Printed in the United States of America, North Mankato, Minnesota.

052015

092015

 THIS BOOK CONTAINS RECYCLED MATERIALS

Photo Credits: iStock, Shutterstock

Production Contributors: Teddy Borth, Jennie Forsberg, Grace Hansen

Design Contributors: Laura Rask, Dorothy Toth

Library of Congress Control Number: 2014958550

Cataloging-in-Publication Data

Hansen, Grace.

 Minerals / Grace Hansen.

  p. cm. -- (Geology rocks!)

ISBN 978-1-62970-907-9

Includes index.

1. Minerals--Juvenile literature.   I. Title.

549--dc23

                    2014958550

Table of Contents

What are Minerals?

Minerals are made naturally.

They are made up of elements.

Living things cannot make minerals. A pearl is a **gem**. A pearl is not a mineral. An oyster makes a pearl.

Mineral Shapes

All minerals form crystals.

There are six crystal shapes.

cubic

tetragonal

orthorhombic

triclinic

hexagonal

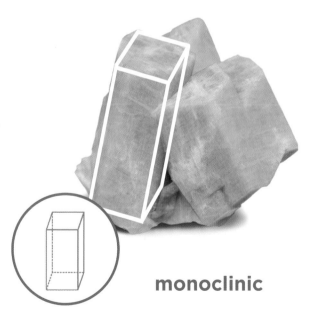

monoclinic

9

Where Minerals Form

Minerals form in the main rock types. They form in **igneous rocks**. Mica forms in these rocks.

mica

11

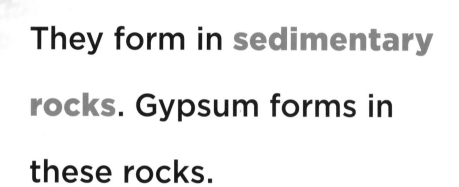

They form in **sedimentary rocks**. Gypsum forms in these rocks.

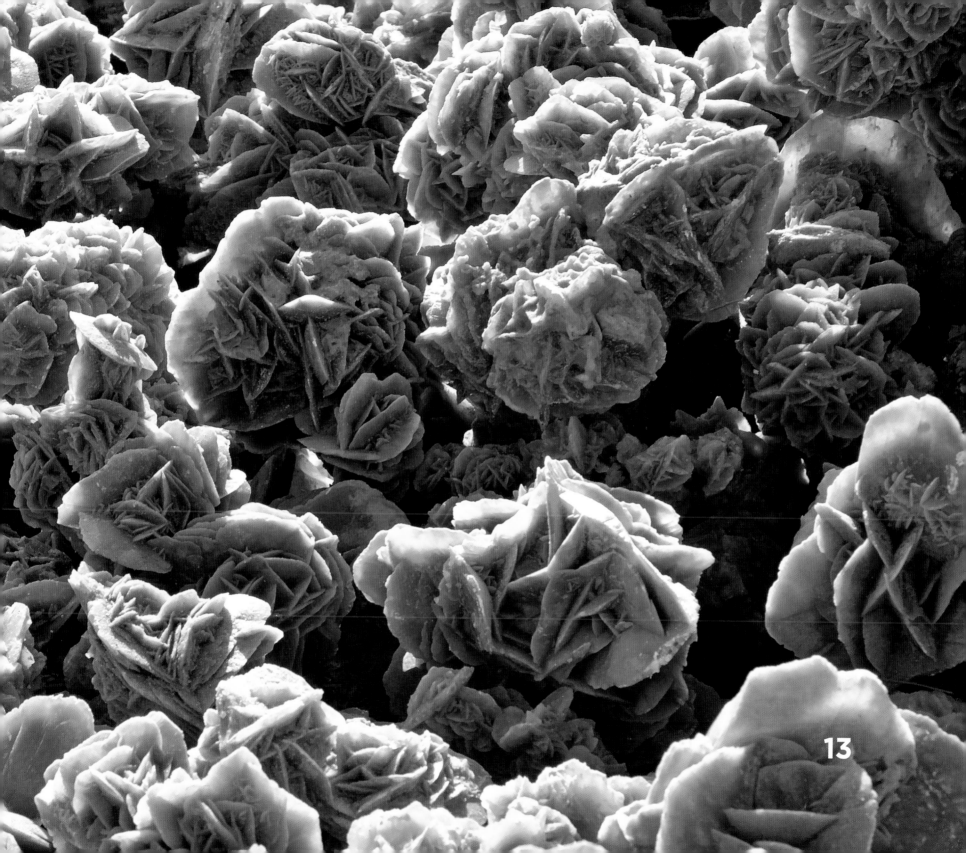

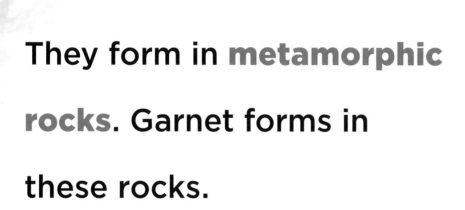

They form in **metamorphic rocks**. Garnet forms in these rocks.

15

Minerals All Around!

Minerals are all around us.

We use them every day.

graphite

Water forms minerals.

Water can freeze or dry up.

Minerals from the water are

left over. Halite can form

this way. Halite makes salt.

halite

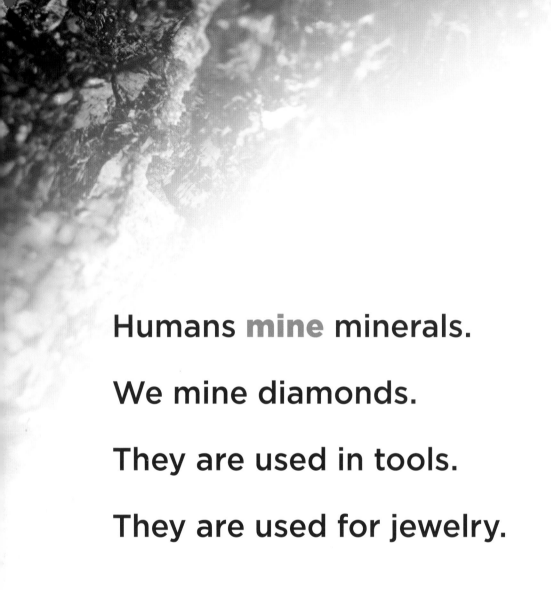

Humans **mine** minerals.

We mine diamonds.

They are used in tools.

They are used for jewelry.

diamond

Mineral Types

apatite **feldspar** **quartz**

azurite **fluorite** **sulfur**

calcite **malachite** **topaz**

Glossary

element – An element is an atom. Atoms make up almost everything on Earth. Minerals are made up of one or more elements. And rocks are made up of one or more minerals.

gem – a valuable stone that is cut, polished, and used in jewelry.

igneous rock – rock formed by the cooling and solidifying of magma or lava.

metamorphic rock – rock that was once one form of rock but has changed to a different rock from heat and pressure.

mine – dig in earth for minerals.

sedimentary rock – rock that has formed from many tiny pieces of rocks.

Index

abdokids.com

Use this code to log on to abdokids.com and access crafts, games, videos, and more!

Abdo Kids Code:
GMK9079